FAITH WALK

FAITH WALK

My Father's Story

Alma J. Evans-Fanniel

FAITH WALK
MY FATHER'S STORY

Some of the names in this book have been changed to protect the privacy of certain individuals.

iUniverse books may be ordered through booksellers or by contacting:

iUniverse
1663 Liberty Drive
Bloomington, IN 47403
www.iuniverse.com
844-349-9409

ISBN: 978-1-6632-0079-2 (sc)
ISBN: 978-1-6632-0078-5 (e)

Library of Congress Control Number: 2020917628

Print information available on the last page.

iUniverse rev. date: 10/14/2020

This book is dedicated to my parents, Reverend Lon Evans and Mary Esther Evans, and my entire family.

I can do all things through Christ which strengtheneth me.
—Philippians 4:13

Contents

Acknowledgments

I would like to express my gratitude to my Lord and Savior Jesus Christ for giving me the vision to write this book, *Faith Walk: My Father's Story.*

This book would not have been possible without the help and guidance of my brother Superintendent Johnnie Evans Sr., as well as my other siblings, Superintendent C. D. Evans, Mellova Joyce Evans-Davis, JoAnn Evans-Weatherspoon, Syretta Evans, and JoNell Evans-Braggs. My thanks to each of you for your encouragement and support. I would like to acknowledge my deceased brother, Saul Evans, and deceased sisters Ruby Jewel Evans-Hall and Doris Ray Evans-Dixon.

I offer special thanks to my husband, Bishop Frank E. Fanniel Sr., and to my children Lanell, Frank Jr., Prettice (Sylvia), and Michael (Pamela). I am also thankful for all the love and support that my grandchildren have displayed throughout this writing process. Many thanks to my granddaughter Mikala, who served as my editorial assistant and provided secretarial support, enthusiasm, patience, and helpful ideas that helped bring this book to its completion.

To book coach Daphine Priscilla Brown-Jack and your assistant, daughter Zoe Jack, thank you for your insight and encouragement. Lastly, thank you, Geraldine Gibson and Pastor Hewett Richardson Jr. for editing the manuscript of *Faith Walk* in preparation for printing.

Foreword

As I grew up in the Church of God in Christ, I remember as a young girl being intrigued by Mother Fanniel. She played the guitar, but most of all, she had a lot in common with my mother. They were very good friends, pastors' wives, and women of *strong* faith. That influenced not only my faith but also my lifestyle.

In early 2019, I was approached by Mother Fanniel to assist her in writing a book. I was excited and honored that she would even think of me to do so.

As we began the journey, I was eager to get to know who she was as a woman of God and also her family dynamic and upbringing, in order to create a story that would have an impact on the world. The story of her father was so intriguing, and he was a true man of God who used his faith in the way that God intended. He was a true servant of God. These factors played a part in naming the book *Faith Walk*.

As you read this book, you will understand and internalize the anointing that was deeply bestowed upon Reverend Lon Evans.

As Mother Fanniel wrote this and we took our journey together, the scripture that came to mind was Matthew 19:26 (NIV): "Jesus looked at them and said, With man this is impossible, but with God all things are possible."

Through *Faith Walk*, you will see that there was nothing less than *possible*!

—Daphine Priscilla Brown-Jack
Author of *The Other Side of the Story*

Preface

The purpose of this book is to highlight the legacy and life of Reverend Lon Evans. This book will give you a snapshot of his work as a minister and pastor, as well as a glimpse of his impact as a husband and father. You will go on many journeys that show the importance of action supported by faith. The story written within these pages will openly display the heart, mind, and soul of a man who truly believed in the healing power of God, as told by his daughter Alma J. Evans-Fanniel. In this book, you will learn about and meet a man who never forgot his true purpose as a servant of God. It is my prayer that this book will help you value the importance of dedication to God, and that it may also serve as a testament to how powerful we can be when we trust, believe, and work with God's purpose and plan for our lives. Come along with me as I share his life and story with you.

Introduction

Reverend Lon Evans was a man who walked by faith. He experienced many challenges and hardships throughout his life, but it was through his faith that he persevered. Even when the odds were heavily against him, he stood secured upon his faith. From the near death of his baby girl to a life-threating situation in which a man put a shotgun to his head and demanded that he denounce his faith, Reverend Lon Evans held firm to his conviction.

As we walk through this journey called life, we are faced with various challenges, obstacles, and struggles. We often quote Hebrews 11:1: "Now faith is the substance of things hoped for, the evidence of things not seen." But how often do we exercise our faith, or better yet, put it into action? When we walk by faith, we don't depend on what we can see; instead, we walk where there is no path or bridge in sight. As Paul reminds us, "For we walk by faith and not by sight" (2 Corinthians 5:7).

It is easy to believe this scripture when our days are filled with love, joy, and happiness, but what do we do about the days filled with much difficulty and misfortune? Will we allow our problems or hindrances to diminish our faith completely? Or will we continue to believe and trust that God will bring us out of the situation victoriously? If we allow our faith to be diminished, then how do we expect to please God? Paul made it clear in Hebrews 11:6: "But without faith it is impossible to please him; for he that cometh to God must believe that he is, and that he is a rewarder of them that diligently seek him." Even though challenges may try to defeat us, obstacles try to block us, and struggles come to restrain and slow us down, by our faith in God we can conquer all our adversities. Sometimes our days are filled with so much darkness that we wonder if there will ever be another sunny day. Yes, our days may be dark, and sometimes we can't see our way, but we have to keep the faith and press forward, for there is a brighter day ahead!

Our faith may not be as great as we desire, but we must not forget that our faith can be the size of a mustard seed and yet have the power to move mountains. We must never forget that we have not made it this far in life on our own. Instead, we have come this far by faith, leaning and depending on our Lord and Savior Jesus Christ. He is a trustworthy guide.

CHAPTER 1

The Unknown Journey

For I know the thoughts that I think toward you, saith the Lord,
thoughts of peace, and not of evil, to give you an expected end.
—Jeremiah 29:11

On February 14, 1886, in the wooded areas of Leon County, Texas, a male child was born and named Lon. His mother and father, who were not married, came from two different races. Like his father, Lon had a fair complexion and blue eyes. At his birth, his mother gave her son her last name. But that was not to last, for while Lon was still very young, his father took ownership of him and changed his last name to Evans, the name of his own father. Lon's father wanted his son to carry his last name, rather than the last name of his mother. Thus began the life and identity of my father, Lon Evans.

As Lon grew up, he maintained a relationship with his mother, even though he was reared by his father. As much as she could, all along the way, Lon's mother watched over him and cared for him during his childhood and preteen years. She was quite concerned about his well-being and uncertain about what would happen to her son. During his younger years, Lon had to adapt to a new way of living. He noted that his father did things differently from his mother, and he found it challenging to adjust to his father and his family.

While living with his father, Lon had to learn many things, such as behaving respectfully and exercising good manners. One night while at the dinner table, Lon ate his food far too quickly, so his father used this inappropriate behavior as a teachable moment to enlighten him about proper etiquette and table manners. Even though some expectations came to be less important to Lon as he grew up, these foundational principles of appropriate behavior would serve him well as he raised his own children.

As it did for many young boys, sports held an important place in Lon's heart and mind. Baseball was his favorite sport, offering Lon an opportunity to feel confident about himself and his abilities. An excellent pitcher, Lon played on the community baseball team, and people from all over would come to their games. He seemed to have a natural gift for baseball, and when we were growing up, he would tell us, "Yeah, people loved coming to see me pitch."

On a more serious note, Lon's father encouraged him to pursue all educational opportunities available to him. Lon attended public school only briefly, but if he had been allowed to continue, he probably would have excelled as a student. Unfortunately, at that time in US history, black children did not have the same opportunities to attend school as white children. Lon was so fair skinned that he did not appear black, so he was initially allowed into public school. But when it was realized that Lon was actually a black child, after only eight days of school attendance, he was forced to leave. After that, he was limited to whatever academic education, skills, and trades he could learn from home.

Fortunately, a kind lady that was a school-teacher, regularly went to Lon's home and taught him to read and write. Today, this is known as homeschooling. While Lon was being educated at home, his father also taught him carpentry, which would eventually become how Lon made his living. In addition to carpentry, he mastered cooking, farming, and several other trades and skills. Lon took what he learned from his academic opportunities and other training, and coupled it with wisdom and common sense. These teachings and trainings would enhance his well-being, both natural and spiritual, as he began his faith walk.

CHAPTER 2

A Personal Encounter

And straightway the father of the child cried out, and said
with tears, Lord, I believe; help thou mine unbelief.
—Mark 9:24

As Lon began to mature into a young man, he was able to use the skills that his father taught him. He used his carpentry skills to rebuild and restore houses that needed roof repairs, leveling, and many other interior and exterior repairs and improvements. These jobs allowed him to provide financially for his biological mother and family.

Lon was growing up to be a responsible young man who made sure his family was financially secure, but his faith in God was yet to be activated. Even though Lon had a Methodist background, he did not have a strong belief in the so-called Holiness movement that everyone was talking about at that time. Everyone, including his friends, was talking about a church revival during which the preacher would lay his hands on someone's head and the person would fall out on the floor. It was said that people were clapping, jumping around, shouting, dancing, and praising God.

Though curious, Lon wasn't convinced. He told his friends, "Aww, those folks ain't real. They don't have anything." But then he heard a voice within him say, "If they don't have anything, neither do you." So he decided to go by the small white church where the revival services were being held and see if there was any truth in what his friends and others were saying. Here is Lon's account of his personal encounter from that night, which changed his life forever:

One night, I decided to go by this church revival just to see if what my friends were saying had any truth. As I began to approach this small white building, I heard a sound like a lot of folks full of excitement. The closer I got to the church, the louder the sound grew. I peeped through the window and saw people falling out all over the floor, and I thought they were going crazy. Then I recognized my friends, and they too were falling out on the floor. I just knew they didn't have anything, because of the way they would carry on and act all the time. Something strange was happening here, and I didn't quite understand it.

As I began to try to walk away, something kept pulling me in the direction to go inside the church. I was trying to resist, but I could not seem to have enough strength to pull myself the opposite way. So I went inside and sat on the back pew. As I sat there, I was in a daze and completely confused about what was happening. I was still in shock of what I saw, with everyone on the floor. I still had no reason for why I was there. I sat there watching all these people doing these strange things.

The preacher began to walk the floor and ask, "Who wants to be saved? For the Bible says come out of your sins and leave them alone." I was still not understanding what was going on. The preacher opened up an altar call. Having this fear on the inside, I got up to head toward the door to leave, but something turned me to go to the altar. The preacher then put his hands on my head. I did not know why he was touching me. When the preacher put his hand on my head, I fell to the floor.

People came and stood over and around me. From that point on, all I could hear was everyone saying, "Jesus, Jesus, Jesus." As they were saying this over me, I began to repeat what they were saying, and I began to feel something I had never felt before in my life. It felt refreshing, like electricity shocking my body, and before I knew it, Christ came into my life and I was filled with the baptism of the Holy Ghost.

I opened my eyes and began to get off the floor, and the preacher looked me in my eyes and said, "God said he wants you to work for him." I was still trying to understand what had just happened to me and the feeling I had just encountered. But now what exactly did he mean that God wants me to work for him? The pastor and the prayer band came to me and told me that since my life had changed, there were things I could and could not do.

Lon's life was transformed that night in that small white church during that revival service. He left refreshed and renewed, but there was one thing that Lon Evans pondered.

CHAPTER 3

Understanding His New Journey

Therefore if any man be in Christ, he is a new creature: old
things are passed away; behold, all things are become new.
—2 Corinthians 5:17

The next morning, Lon was sitting on the side of his bed, reminiscing about all the things that had occurred the previous night. More importantly, he thought about what the pastor had said about what he could and could not do. His first thought was about giving up his beloved baseball, and how he was going to tell his friends. During those times, the saints considered playing sports worldly.

Today, we may think this idea is somewhat bizarre, but they believed that saved and sanctified people should not do the things that unsaved people did. They considered worldly things unclean, based on the scripture "Wherefore come out from among them, and be ye separate, saith the Lord, and touch not the unclean thing; and I will receive you" (2 Corinthians 6:17). They believed that once you were saved and Christ became the center of your life, you shouldn't want to do what the world was doing. As a new creature in Christ, your old desires should be overshadowed by your new desires for Christ.

Lon obeyed and gave up his beloved baseball to follow and do the will of Christ. As the days went by, he adjusted to his new life and being saved. The pastor and prayer band taught him how to live a saved life and not surrender to the things of the flesh. Lon wanted to make sure he did everything right in the sight of God, and he thought that God didn't want him to have a life outside the church. But in the back of his mind, Lon was still thinking, *No more baseball?*

One day Lon heard about the new pitcher who would be taking his position on the baseball team. He was eager to see this new pitcher, and more importantly, Lon wondered if the new person was a better pitcher than he was. Unable to suppress his curiosity, Lon finally decided to go to the game, just to get a glimpse of his replacement. He didn't want anyone to notice that he was there, so he hid behind a large tree that was far away from the crowd at the game. "Can a man hide himself in hiding places so I do not see him, declares the Lord" (Jeremiah 23:24 NASB). Lon was fighting his conscience regarding what he had been told by the preacher about baseball, but believing that nobody would know that he was there, he stayed to watch the game.

During the game, an unusual incident took place. One batter hit the ball so hard that it flew beyond the outfield, and everyone watched to see how far it would travel. Lon saw that the ball was heading straight toward his hiding place, and before he knew what was happening, the ball hit him in the head and knocked him to the ground. He tried to get up, but he didn't have enough strength to do so. Everyone came running to see who had been hit by the ball. As they came closer, they realized that it was Lon and began yelling, "Is that Lon who got hit? I thought he was saved and couldn't come to the game!"

Lon was extremely embarrassed, and a huge lump was forming on his forehead, but he had learned that you can never hide from God. "For My eyes are on all their ways; they are not hidden from My face, nor is their iniquity concealed from My eyes" (Jeremiah 16:17 NASB).

A few nights later, feeling condemned within his heart, Lon told the pastor all that had happened on that day. The pastor told Lon to apologize to the church for disobeying God's word. Lon obeyed the pastor, repented to God, and apologized before the congregation. Then he felt better and was ready for a fresh start in his new life.

CHAPTER 4

Recognizing God's Voice

Also I heard the voice of the Lord, saying, whom shall I send,
and who will go for us? Then said I, here am I; send me.
—Isaiah 6:8

After repenting and getting back on track, Lon began growing
spiritually and understanding the life of being saved and filled with
the Holy Ghost. During one Sunday morning service, the pastor said
to Lon, "God has something for you to do." Lon had no idea what the
pastor meant by that. However, Lon would pray to God about anything
and everything, so he began praying for understanding of what the
pastor had said to him.

One hot day while working in the sugarcane fields, Lon became so
overheated that he fell to the ground and couldn't get up. While lying
on the ground, he heard a voice say over and over, "I have work for you
to do." Like the experience of Saul, Lon was helpless on the ground
and at the mercy of a great God (Acts 9:6–9). He answered, "Yes, Lord,
I will do whatever you want me to do." After accepting God's call, he
felt the cool breath of God and knew he was ready for the task that
God had given him.

At the next church service, Lon got up and joyfully told the
congregation about the encounter that he had had with God the

previous day. He told the congregation that he was ready to go wherever and do whatever God wanted him to.

Being a young man in his thirties, Reverend Lon Evans had accepted his call to the ministry and to preaching the gospel. As the years passed, he began to listen more and more to the voice of the Lord. One day the Lord told him, "Go to Midway, Texas, and stop where I tell you to stop."

Reverend Lon had never been to Midway. He knew that it was thirty miles or so from where he lived, but he didn't know in which direction. Neither did he have any means of transportation or know anyone who lived in Midway. However, Lon didn't allow these few challenges to prevent him from doing the work God had for him. He had enough faith and trust in God to know that the Holy Ghost would lead and guide him in the right direction. As the scripture encourages us, "Trust in the Lord with all thine heart; and lean not unto thine own understanding. In all thy ways acknowledge him, and he shall direct thy paths" (Proverbs 3:5–6).

Obedient to God's voice and led by the Holy Ghost, Reverend Lon began walking from where he lived in Leon County, Texas. Along the way, a car pulled up beside him and a man leaned out the window and asked, "Where are you going?" When Reverend Lon replied that he was trying to get to a town called Midway, the man said, "That's a long way to walk." The man offered Reverend Lon a ride, so Reverend Lon got into the car and traveled as far as the man could take him. When he got out of the car, he was close enough to walk the remaining distance to Midway, Texas.

CHAPTER 5

Activating His Faith

So then faith cometh by hearing, and hearing by the word of God.
—Romans 10:17

In 1929, after arriving in Midway, Reverend Lon faced more challenges. He was in a new place, but he had no money and lacked most of the essentials needed to survive. One day, Reverend Lon was led by the Holy Ghost to a sizable community in which many people lived. There was no church or preacher in the area, but there were many souls in need of salvation. "Therefore said he unto them, the harvest truly is great, but the laborers are few: pray ye therefore the Lord of the harvest, that he would send forth laborers into his harvest" (Luke 10:2). As Reverend Lon became familiar with the area, God told him that this was the place where He wanted him to be.

As the days went by, Reverend Lon met a white gentleman named Mr. W. who lived in the community. They began to talk, and as they became better acquainted, Reverend Lon shared with Mr. W. that he was a minister of the gospel. Because Mr. W. knew practically everyone in the area, he wondered if Reverend Lon was truthful about being a minister. As they continued talking, Reverend Lon told Mr. W. where he had traveled from and why he was in Midway. Reverend Lon said that God had wanted him to come there because He had a great work for him to do.

Mr. W. said, "There are a lot of people here. Do you think you can do anything with them? All they know is drinking, smoking, fighting, and gambling."

Reverend Lon replied, "Yes, by the help of the Lord, and if you allow me a chance." As the conversation continued, Reverend Lon spoke of how he was a praying man of faith and that he believed God was a healer. He believed that when he prayed, God answered his prayers.

Mr. W. became captivated by what Reverend Lon was saying about God being a healer. Finally he said, "I have a cow that's been sick for a few days. Could you pray that my cow would get well?" The cow was important to Mr. W.'s family business, so he needed her to get well soon. Reverend Lon agreed, and as Mr. W. continued talking, Reverend Lon walked over to the cow and began to pray that God would heal the animal.

A few days later, as Reverend Lon was walking down the road from Midway, Mr. W. saw him from a distance and recognized him. Mr. W. had exciting news to share with Reverend Lon, and as the two men approached each other, Mr. W. began shouting, "My cow is healed! My cow is healed!" God had answered Reverend Lon's prayer and miraculously healed Mr. W.'s cow. Furthermore, that experience convinced Mr. W. that Reverend Lon was indeed a man of God.

Because Mr. W. was so grateful for the healing of his cow, God touched his heart to show favor toward Reverend Lon. As time passed, Reverend Lon continued to pray and minister to the people of Midway, and the Lord was blessing his ministry. People were being healed, delivered, set free, and saved from their sins, even though Reverend Lon still did not have a place to conduct services. However, help was on the way. God used Mr. W. to assist Reverend Lon by letting him conduct church services on his property.

God touched the hearts of a few of the men who were now saved, and they became deacons and helpers in Reverend Lon's ministry. Reverend Lon called a meeting with them to discuss the plans and actual location on the property for their services. They didn't have the money or resources to construct a building, so Reverend Lon had

Mr. J., one of the deacons, and others build the first church as a brush arbor. A brush arbor is a rough, open-sided shelter constructed of vertical poles driven into the ground, with additional long poles laid across the top as support for a roof of brush, cut branches, or hay. It was a temporary outdoor meeting place where religious services could be held.

The ministry began to expand, more souls were added to the church (Acts 2:47), and in just over a year, the ministry had outgrown the brush arbor. Because of extenuating circumstances, of which I don't know the details, Reverend Lon had to leave and seek out another place to hold services. Fortunately, God had a ram in the bush. One of the brethren of the church offered Reverend Lon the use of a house that he owned, and they began holding church services in there. Once again, God showed Reverend Lon that His stamp of approval was upon his ministry.

Eventually the ministry was blessed by God to purchase lumber and build a church. They didn't have property on which to build, but God once again worked through Mr. W., who allowed them to put the church on his property. In this building, the Lord performed  many miracles, signs, and wonders. People came from all over to witness the mighty hand of God. They would arrive sick and leave healed, or arrive bound by the devil's hand and leave set free by the power of God. Oh yes, they left that place different from how they came, in Jesus's name!

CHAPTER 6

A Dream Becomes a Reality

Whoso findeth a wife findeth a good thing,
and obtaineth favor of the Lord.
—Proverbs 18:22

The Lord had blessed the ministry and work of Reverend Lon Evans. The church was built, the congregation was growing, and most of all, souls were being added to God's kingdom. However, there was still a void, something missing in his life. Reverend Lon was married in his early years but the details of that union are not disclosed in this book. After the death of his first wife, Reverend Lon remained a single man for more than six years. He desired to have a special woman by his side—a woman who would understand the call that God had on his life and be devoted to God herself. When we please and give ourselves to the Lord, He will bless us with our heart's desires (Psalm 37:4). Since Reverend Lon was a man of prayer who needed a wife, God gave him his heart's desire. "Don't worry about anything; instead, pray about everything. Tell God what you need, and thank him for all he has done" (Philippians 4:6 NLT).

As Reverend Lon prayed, God heard the request of his servant. One night as Reverend Lon was sleeping, he had a dream in which God showed him a beautiful young lady with a fair complexion. God said, "This is the wife for whom you have been asking." We can only imagine the great joy and encouragement that Reverend Lon felt, knowing that God had heard his prayer and given him a view of his future wife. Some people might consider Reverend Lon's dream experience to be wishful thinking or wonder if anything tangible would result from such a dream. We must not forget that sometimes our imagination, our dreams, and even our prayers are a foretaste of what is about to become reality in our lives.

A few days after his dream, Reverend Lon conducted a revival service, and afterward he went to fellowship with the people from the service. As he shook hands and greeted the saints, he noticed a familiar face across the room. The face was that of the young lady whom God had shown him in his dream a few nights earlier. He stood in amazement and disbelief that she was physically there before his eyes. He went up to the young lady, who was accompanied by her mother, and greeted them. Trying not to be hasty and get ahead of himself, he then left the church and went on his way.

Later, while attending another church service, Reverend Lon looked around and saw the same young lady and her mother. He told his friend Brother Mat, "I dreamed that this young lady is going to be my wife."

Brother Mat didn't believe him and said, "Lon, you should be ashamed of yourself. She's too young for you."

After the service, Reverend Lon went up and introduced himself to the young lady, Mary Esther Alexander, and her mother, Stella Alexander. After a brief conversation with them, Reverend Lon left for the evening, once again reassured that God had a plan and was working to enrich and fulfill his life.

As God ordained it, Reverend Lon and Mary Esther would see each other again and again. As they slowly got to know each other, Reverend Lon told Mrs. Alexander about the

dream he had of her daughter becoming his wife. He told her that he had prayed to God for a wife, and that in his dream, the Lord had showed Mary Esther to him as that person. He told Mrs. Alexander that the first time he had seen Mary Esther, he had realized that she was the young lady from his dream.

Mrs. Alexander asked Reverend Lon if he was sure that it was Mary Esther whom God had shown him. He continued to talk with her, and eventually she became convinced. "If God showed her to you," she told Reverend Lon, "I have no choice but to take your word for it. Make sure you take care of my daughter."

Reverend Lon replied, "Yes, I will." He left full of amazement and wonder at how God had provided a wife for him. The Lord had once again answered his prayers and given him favor to express his sincere thoughts to the mother of his soon-to-be wife. This had allowed Mrs. Alexander to give her blessing willingly and her daughter to him, knowing that this was the plan of God.

A few days later, Reverend Lon went to Mrs. Alexander's home to pick up his future bride and take her to the courthouse. Once there, they went before the justice of the peace and were united in holy matrimony. They were now Mr. Lon and Mrs. Mary Esther Evans. Their new life had begun!

And so God laid the foundation for the coming together of the two people who would eventually become parents to my siblings and me. The marriage of Lon and Mary was just the beginning of many memorable years of happy union, complete with children to carry on their spiritual and natural legacy. Mary Esther proved to be a special woman who understood the importance of being by her husband's side. Reverend Lon had found a woman who understood the call that God had on his life and was willing to surrender herself to God also. Yes, his dream became a reality!

CHAPTER 7

A Moment of Silence

Verily, verily, I say unto you, that ye shall weep and
lament, but the world shall rejoice: and ye shall be
sorrowful, but your sorrow shall be turned into joy.
—John 16:20

Reverend Lon had married the woman of his dreams, and she was already saved and filled with the Holy Ghost. He took her home and introduced her to his family, church members, and friends in the community. He was proud to be married to Mary Evans, and sometimes he would speak so highly of her that she would get bashful and shy. He would say to her, "You are so pretty. You are beautiful." Oh yes, that was his Mae, and he loved her as Christ loved the church (Ephesians 5:25).

As the years passed, God continued to bless them and their marriage. They were operating the ministry that God had given them while also fulfilling God's command to be fruitful, multiply, and replenish the earth (Genesis 1:28). After being blessed with four children, Mae was once again pregnant.

When the day arrived for the new baby to be born, Mae was in pain and having frequent contractions, while Reverend Lon stood across the room ecstatic to be having another baby. As Mae's labor progressed, Reverend Lon sent the other children to stay with the neighbors. Day became evening, and Mae was still in labor, groaning and moaning in despair. Reverend Lon took her hand and began praying for her. There came a silence, and then suddenly the sound of a baby crying loudly. Their baby boy had made his arrival into the world.

After a few seconds, there came another moment of silence. The baby had stopped crying, which worried the midwife. She realized that he was no longer breathing, and although she tried over and over again to restore his breathing, the Evans baby boy was dead.

When the children returned, they were excited to meet their new baby brother. They entered the house asking where he was, and their father had to gather them together and tell them the sad news. He reluctantly told them that their baby brother had gone to be with Jesus, and the children were devastated.

As young children usually do, they had lots of questions. One child asked, "He went with Jesus already? What was his name?"

Reverend Lon told them that his name was Saul.

Then one of the girls asked, "Is he coming back with Jesus?"

With hesitation and grief, Reverend Lon replied, "No, baby girl, he is not."

This was a deep tragedy for the Evans family, and their hearts were heavy from the loss of their baby boy, Saul. What an emotional trauma the family must have experienced that day. They had gone from great excitement and expectation to a place of loss and tears. Later that day, little Saul's body was laid to rest. But even in the midst of their grief, somehow the Evans family held on to their faith in God.

CHAPTER 8

God's Divine Protection

No weapon that is formed against thee shall prosper.
—Isaiah 54:17

As the family began to heal from the loss of little baby Saul, Reverend Lon and Mae continued to walk by faith. The ministry began to call for him to travel more, conducting revivals and services in various communities. People were being healed and delivered by the power of God as the Lord worked through Reverend Lon in a mighty way.

Reverend Lon always wanted Mae to travel with him in the ministry, but she was unable to do so when the children were still young and in school. Also, it would have been difficult to travel with the children at certain times of the year because of rain or snow. But even though Mae wasn't able to be with her husband in person, she was always with him in spirit. She would constantly pray for traveling grace and protection, but also for God to bless the ministry. Reverend Lon always knew that Mae was the right woman for him, standing right by his side and supporting him in the ministry for God's kingdom.

It was Reverend Lon's desire to be home with his wife and family as their protector and provider. But God had work for him to do, and he knew that God would take care of his family while he was away. As he prayed for God's protection over his family, the enemy was plotting to do harm to him. The devil knew that Reverend Lon was faithful to

God and committed to his God-given assignment. If he couldn't stop Reverend Lon from doing God's work, then he would try to kill him.

One day, on his way to pray for someone, Reverend Lon came to a point in the road where he could take a shortcut through the woods and shorten his journey. As he walked through the woods, he noticed a man on a horse hiding behind a tree. The man appeared to be waiting for Reverend Lon, who just continued walking, unafraid because he knew that God was with him. "Fear thou not; for I am with thee: be not dismayed; for I am thy God: I will strengthen thee; yea, I will help thee; yea, I will uphold thee with the right hand of my righteousness" (Isaiah 41:10).

Then the man rode his horse out from behind the tree and said, "I heard about you and what you're doing. All this shaking and jerking. I know you're not all about what you preach, so here, drink this whiskey."

Knowing that God was with him, Reverend Lon looked at the man and said, "No, I'm not a drinker, and I won't turn my back on God for a drink."

The man pulled out a gun and pointed it at Reverend Lon's head. "You'd better drink this whiskey, or I'll shoot you right here."

Reverend Lon said to the man in a forceful voice, "I'd rather die than drink that and lie."

As Reverend Lon spoke, the man suddenly fell off his horse, and the fully loaded gun slipped from his hands. Now lying on the ground, the man was unable to move or speak.

Feeling no ill will toward the man, Reverend Lon was led by the Holy Ghost to assist him in his helpless condition. Now convinced that Reverend Lon was real, the man was afraid and didn't want anything else to do with this preacher. Reverend Lon helped the man back to his feet, but then the man told Reverend Lon to continue on his way.

Because of Reverend Lon's faith and love for God, he could count on God to protect him from all harm. "The Lord will keep you from all harm, he will watch over your life; the Lord will watch over your coming and going both now and forevermore" (Psalm 121:7–8 NIV).

CHAPTER 9

Doubt to Belief

And straightway the father of the child cried out, and said
with tears, Lord, I believe; help thou mine unbelief.
—Mark 9:24

God had performed miracle after miracle through his servant Reverend Lon Evans, and greater miracles were yet to come. The news of God's miraculous healings was spreading throughout the community like wildfire. Reverend Lon constantly prayed to be in accordance with what God would have him do.

As he asked for God's direction, God instructed him to organize a prayer team to accompany him. Without any question, that's exactly what Reverend Lon did. Just as God told Jeremiah to call for the mourning women, Reverend Lon gathered five to six women to travel with him when he was doing God's business. "Thus saith the Lord of hosts, consider ye, and call for the mourning women, that they may come; and send for cunning women, that they may come" (Jeremiah 9:17). As Reverend Lon ministered, prayer team members would read scripture and sing Zion's songs. Reverend Lon now had prayer warriors to accompany him in doing kingdom work.

One day in 1950 when Reverend Lon was at home, he noticed a deacon from the church running frantically toward his house. From the man's gestures, Reverend Lon knew that there was an emergency. He stepped outside to greet the deacon and asked, "What's wrong?"

Out of breath, the deacon replied, "My niece was playing outside when she accidentally swallowed a large, sharp nail." The deacon hadn't known who to go, but he had faith in his pastor, Reverend Lon, and believed in God for a miracle. With concern, Reverend Lon and the deacon left in haste to attend to the little girl.

When they arrived at the child's home, her father approached Reverend Lon with a look of uncertainty on his face. With a trembling voice, he explained what had happened. They had already been to the hospital, where the doctor had told them there was nothing to be done because the hospital didn't have the proper medical equipment. His only instructions to the girl's parents had been to hope that she would pass the nail through a bowel movement within a few days.

Looking at the nervous little girl, Reverend Lon encouraged the family and said, "The Lord will work it out."

The mother and father looked at Reverend Lon in disbelief. Perhaps they believed in God and had heard of the miracles being performed, but a positive outcome for a situation like this just seemed impossible. Their belief was turning to doubt, and when doubt exists in our lives, it further diminishes our belief. If only they had known that nothing is impossible for God. Just as the scriptures declared in Mark 9:23, "Jesus said unto him, If thou canst believe, all things are possible to him that believeth."

Reverend Lon continued encouraging the little girl and her parents. He told them that he and the prayer team were going to fast and pray for three days, believing the nail would pass from the little girl's body.

As the days went by, they fasted and prayed without ceasing (Acts 12:5). During this time, the nail remained inside the little girl, but God was still at work. For one thing, He did not allow the nail to move around inside the little girl's stomach, which could have caused pain and irreparable damage. Furthermore, the little girl was able to eat without discomfort, and she showed no sign of fear. Because of her behavior, some people began to think that maybe the nail was no longer in her stomach, but her parents knew that it was still there.

On the third day, Reverend Lon received the miraculous news that the little girl had passed the nail through a bowel movement. Once again, God had heard and answered the prayers of the saints. Although the earthly doctor didn't have the equipment necessary to help the little girl, the Great Physician knew just what to do. God always has a remedy.

The little girl's father was so astonished by the miracle that God performed that he became a member of the church, where Reverend Lon served as pastor.

CHAPTER 10

A Miracle Moment

As soon as Jesus heard the word that was spoken, he saith unto
the ruler of the synagogue, be not afraid, only believe.
—Mark 5:36

Many years had now passed since the death of little baby Saul, and the Evans family had been blessed with additional children, four beautiful daughters. God had actually given them more than they had lost, similar to Job chapter 42, in which God blesses Job with a double return of what he had lost. When blessings come our way, we should expect attacks from the devil. Even so, no matter what the enemy throws our way, we know that he can do no more than God allows. God takes what the enemy means for evil and turns it around for our good.

On a midsummer day, Reverend Lon and his older children were out in the field working, while Mae was at home with Mellova, their two-year-old baby girl. Mae was cooking so that the family would have something to eat upon their return home, and the baby energetically played on the floor. At some point, Mae realized that the baby was no longer in the kitchen, and she began to frantically search the house. From room to room she went, until finally she opened the door to the back porch and saw her baby lying there.

Mae screamed, "Oh God, help us, Lord!" She picked the baby up, noticing immediately that Mellova was limp and lethargic. Holding the baby, she smelled a strong odor, and she looked around and saw an open bottle of cleaning solvent tipped over. This solvent was harmful to the eyes, the nose if inhaled, to the skin, and deadly if swallowed. Questions immediately ran through Mae's mind: *Did the baby swallow some of that liquid? If so, how much? What should I do?* The scariest question, of course, was whether the baby girl was going to be all right.

Minutes later, Reverend Lon and the children arrived home and heard Mae screaming. As they ran inside, Mae stood there holding the baby in her arms. When she explained what had happened, Reverend Lon immediately grabbed Mellova and told Mae that he needed to take the baby to the doctor. He took one of his older daughters with him.

By the time they arrived at the doctor's office, the baby was panting and her breath was short. After examining the baby, the doctor told Reverend Lon, "Sorry, Lon, but you need to take her back home. There's nothing else I can do for her."

As they drove back home, the baby stopped panting and her breath became very faint. Reverend Lon asked his daughter to hold her baby sister in her arms and check to see if she was still breathing. She told her father, "No, Daddy, she's not breathing."

Upon arriving home, Reverend Lon went into the house and told Mae that he was going to spend the night alone with the baby. He took Mellova and went in the room, and the family knew not to disturb or interrupt him. The other children went to bed with heavy hearts, wondering if they would have a baby sister the next morning. Reverend Lon stayed in the room all night, praying to God for a miracle.

Early the next morning, Reverend Lon came out of the room with a very energetic and playful little girl, alive and full of laughter. Reverend Lon, full of joy, said, "Mae, here's our baby!" Everyone was thrilled as they witnessed the baby girl jumping, laughing, and playing as if nothing bad had happened the previous day.

God had worked a wonderful miracle. Just as Jesus had raised Jairus's daughter from the dead, that same healing power raised the Evans family's little baby girl from the claws of death. Reverend Lon and Mae thanked God mightily for His divine healing.

CHAPTER 11

Reverend Lon Evans's Points for Wisdom

If any of you lack wisdom, let him ask of God, that giveth to all
men liberally, and upbraided not; and it shall be given him.
—James 1:5

As Reverend Lon listened to God, he was given eleven points of
wisdom:

- In all your getting, get understanding (Proverbs 4:7).
- Watch how you carry yourself (1 Timothy 4:16).
- Never let the devil know your testimony or your next step (2 Corinthians 2:1).
- Stay in your lane (1 Thessalonians 4:11).
- Know what is in your spiritual life (Matthew 17:19–21).
- Stay on the highway of holiness (Isaiah 35:8).
- Take care of your anointing (Judges 16:20).
- Always keep an updated inventory of your spiritual life (2 Corinthians 13:5).
- Respect God's house (1 Timothy 3:15).
- Anything you sneak or hide, remember God can always see you (Proverbs 15:3).
- Your conscience will always follow you (Hebrews 13:18).

CHAPTER 12

Faith to Favor

For the Lord God is a sun and shield: the Lord will give grace and
glory: no good thing will he withhold from them that walk uprightly.
—Psalm 84:11

God had previously touched the heart of Mr. W. to allow Reverend Lon
and the church members to erect a building on his property, and now
God was again going to show favor to his servant. As the years passed,
a great change had taken place, and the community that had once been
scandalous and unlawful was now moral and respectable.

Mr. W., the man whose sick cow had been healed by Reverend
Lon's prayers, was amazed at the community's turnaround. He had
challenged Reverend Lon's ability to bring about change with the
drinking, fighting, and gambling that had been a way of life when
Reverend Lon had first arrived in the community.

Reverend Lon had replied, "With the help of the Lord, and if you
will give me a chance." Over the years, Reverend Lon had certainly
made a difference, and most community members were now living a
better life through Christ Jesus.

Recognizing Reverend Lon as a true servant of God, Mr. W.'s
heart once again embraced the work of the Lord. God was blessing
the church, and he wanted to show his gratitude to God, so he said to
Reverend Lon, "As long as there is a church on this land, I will deed

you this property." Philippians 4:19 encourages us: "But my God shall supply all your needs according to his riches in glory by Christ Jesus." God did just that when He touched the heart of Mr. W. and made the necessary provisions for His servant. After the land was deeded to Reverend Lon, he named the church Wilson Chapel Holiness Church.

As Reverend Lon continued his travels throughout the communities, he began to fellowship with other churches. One night he went to a district meeting of the Church of God in Christ and met Bishop F. L. Haynes. As the two men became better acquainted, Bishop Haynes recognized the special gift of God upon Reverend Lon.

As they continued to fellowship, Reverend Lon became more interested in the Church of God in Christ. He loved their adherence to holiness and their dedication not only to preaching holiness but also to living a holy life every day. Bishop Haynes told him all about the Church of God in Christ denomination, and Reverend Lon was encouraged by what he heard and witnessed. Even though he had a great desire to become a part of this denomination, he went back to Wilson Chapel to discuss it with the membership.

When Reverend Lon returned to his church the following Sunday and told his members what he had learned and experienced, they agreed to join the Church of God in Christ denomination. Upon their acceptance into the Church of God in Christ, they changed the name of their church to Wilson Chapel Church of God in Christ.

CHAPTER 13

A Cycle of Miracles

Verily, verily, I say unto you, He that believeth on me, the works that
I do shall he do also; and greater works than these shall he do.
—John 14:12

Reverend Lon and the Wilson Chapel Church of God in Christ family
were excited about what the Lord was doing among His people. They
were experiencing the manifestation of God's miraculous blessings.
God was using His servant, Reverend Lon Evans, in ways no one
in that area had previously witnessed. The people were beginning to
believe and expect miracles to take place, no matter how impossible
the situation might seem.

One-day Reverend Lon was at a small grocery store in the
community called the Crossroad. He was having a conversation with a
woman who had been told by her doctor that she had a tumor. As the
woman talked, Reverend Lon had no doubt that God would heal her.
When she finished telling him what her doctor had said, he asked if
she would let him pray for her.

He was surprised when the woman said, "There is nobody living
close enough to the Lord, in this day, to be able to get a prayer through."

Reverend Lon didn't allow her response to change his determination
to pray to the Lord for her healing. All he said was, "Let me try, and
we'll see." He fasted and prayed for the next three days.

Three days later, they saw each other at the same convenience store, but this time there was something different about her. She walked up to Reverend Lon and said with a trembling voice, "I vomited up two gallon buckets of bodily fluids. I don't know what it was, but I could hardly flush it down the toilet." As she continued explaining what had happened to her, she said, "I didn't believe that anyone, in this day and age, could get a powerful prayer through to God. Reverend Lon, the Lord is with you, and I believe he heard your prayer. I am healed."

Reverend Lon didn't take any credit for what God had done. He told her, "Never doubt God. Have faith, because He is a healer." God had once again performed a miracle.

During 1959, Reverend Lon was running a revival at a Baptist church in Lubbock, Texas. After he finished preaching each sermon, he would sing this song:

> I got a new world in my view.
> I am on my journey through.
> I am striving to make it to that promised land.
> It makes no difference what the people say.
> I am going to praise God.
> I have a new world in my view.

Reverend Lon had no issues with other denominations. For him, it was all about one God and the healing and saving of souls.

That night, one of the church members that was blind heard about the service. He wanted to hear this preacher everyone was talking about, so he asked his friends and family to take him. As Reverend Lon was preaching, he noticed a group of people carrying this man into the church. Pausing in the middle of his message, Reverend Lon said, "Put him down." The congregation turned and looked to see who Reverend Lon was talking to. As Reverend Lon stepped down from the pulpit, he said to the blind man, "The Lord is going to heal you tonight, but you must have faith and believe."

Walking toward the sound of Reverend Lon's voice, the blind man replied, "Yes, preacher, I believe." He stopped right in front of

Reverend Lon, who began to pray and anoint him with blessed oil. When Reverend Lon waved his hands in front of the blind man's eyes, the man said, "I see a little shadow." Reverend Lon then grabbed a white towel and waved it in front of the man's eyes once, and the man shouted happily, "I see something white!"

When he said that, the congregation shouted with joy, rejoicing that the man could see again. Reverend Lon laid his hand on the man's eyes and said, "You are already healed. Now you must continue to believe." The man walked out of the church with no assistance.

Twenty years later, that man was still giving his testimony and telling of the goodness of God, how he had once been blind but now could see. The man was able to retire from the company where he had worked for more than twenty years, all because he had faith that God was going to heal him.

As the days went by, Reverend Lon continued his work in the Lord. In 1960, a lady in Midway, Texas, was told by her doctor that she was dying. One day when Reverend Lon was at home, someone came to his house to tell him about that lady's situation. Reverend Lon immediately jumped up to prepare to go to the lady. Taking Johnnie, one of his sons, with him, they drove approximately two to three miles to the lady's home.

Upon arriving, they noticed a man standing on the porch. Reverend Lon looked over at Johnnie and asked, "Son, are you afraid?"

Johnnie replied with a scratchy voice, "Yes."

"What are you afraid of?" Reverend Lon asked.

Johnnie replied, "I'm afraid that you'll get in trouble if something happens to her." Johnnie was a child of wisdom, and he didn't want any charges filed against his father. He didn't know that the doctor had already given this woman up to die.

Reverend Lon told Johnnie, "There's nothing to worry about, son. The doctor already came to this house and did all that he could do for the lady." Johnnie sighed with relief, and they got out of the car. With his son following right behind him, Reverend Lon walked toward the gate of the house and said with authority, "Death, I want you to come out, because my son and I are coming in."

The lady's husband led Reverend Lon and Johnnie into the house and to her bedroom. Walking over to the lady's bedside, Reverend Lon and his son kneeled down and began to pray. During the prayer, Reverend Lon noticed Johnnie looking above the bed.

Johnnie exclaimed, "I saw something falling all around the bed."

Then the woman jumped out of bed and yelled, "Whoa!" She started dancing all around the room and out onto the porch. Once again Reverend Lon's faith was encouraged to see that God was still in the healing business and that He cannot fail.

CHAPTER 14

Blessed Beyond Measure

For God is not unrighteous to forget your work and labor
of love, which ye have shewed toward his name, in that
ye have ministered to the saints, and do minister.
—Hebrews 6:10

In 1961, there was a lady who had a tick bite. Some tick bites are harmless, but apparently this tick was carrying a disease, which it passed to the lady. She began to experience a variety of symptoms, ranging from an infection to swelling in her body. Once again Reverend Lon was called on to pray that God would heal this lady's affliction, and indeed God did heal her. When Reverend Lon prayed for the lady, her husband was at work. When he returned home from work, he knew that a miracle had happened, so he was able to testify about Reverend Lon's prayers and how God healed his wife. When the man had left work, his wife was very sick, but when he returned home, his wife was healed.

Later Reverend Lon met that same man, who was still rejoicing over how God had healed his wife. The man was so grateful for how the Lord had used Reverend Lon to pray for his wife that he said, "I have a large four-room house that I want to give you. You can either move in or tear it down."

Reverend Lon realized that God was blessing him because he had blessed others through his ministry. The Evans family moved into that house, and later Reverend Lon was able to add two more rooms onto it, making the house even more comfortable for his family. Reverend Lon praised God for blessing him and his family with the house. He knew, without a doubt, that he was being rewarded because of his unwavering faith in God.

In 1962, in the community of Leon Prairie County, there was a gentleman who had suffered a stroke. A stroke can leave a person with serious handicaps—difficulties in speaking, diminished eyesight, paralysis or numbness in the face or extremities—and sometimes a stroke results in death. The effects from this man's stroke prevented him from being able to work.

Once again, the man of faith, Reverend Lon, was called upon to pray that God would heal the man. The word of the Lord tells us in James 5:14–16, "Is any sick among you? Let him call for the elders of the church; and let them pray over him, anointing him with oil in the name of the Lord. And the prayer of faith shall save the sick, and the Lord shall raise him up." After Reverend Lon prayed to God to heal this gentleman, all effects of the man's stroke disappeared and he was able to go back to work. Oh, what a miracle the Lord had done.

As time passed, this same gentleman wanted to extend his gratitude and thankfulness to Reverend Lon. He said, "I want to help you out, so I'll allow you to use thirty-three acres of my land to sharecrop for your family." The Lord had once again blessed his servant for his faithfulness to kingdom work. "And all these blessings shall come on thee, and overtake thee, if thou shalt hearken unto the voice of the Lord thy God" (Deuteronomy 28:2). Yes, through his faith walk, commitment, and dedication to God, Reverend Lon was *blessed beyond measure*!

CHAPTER 15

The Cry that Stirred the Minds of the People

Nevertheless I have somewhat against thee,
because thou hast left thy first love.
—Revelation 2:4

As each Sunday passed, Reverend Lon continued in prayer for the saints and preaching the gospel of Jesus Christ. But he became concerned and troubled in his spirit about some things that were happening within the church. The people had become complacent, comfortable, no longer concerned about their relationship with God, and even slack in their attendance.

One fourth Sunday morning, Reverend Lon was at the church early, before any of the members had arrived. He was in consecration on behalf of his concerns for the church and the membership. As he prayed to the empty pews, as though each one was occupied, he heard the sound of a crying baby. Reverend Lon stopped praying for a moment and looked around the sanctuary, but no one was there, so he went outside to search for the source of the emphatic cry.

As Reverend Lon walked around the outside of the church, one of the deacons drove up. Getting out of his car, the deacon heard the sound too, and he asked, "Reverend, do you hear a baby crying?"

Reverend Lon replied, "Yes, I hear it." They both heard the cry, but they never could find where the cry of the baby was coming from. This was a very unusual situation, so Reverend Lon began to pray.

Later that evening, Reverend Lon was preparing for bed, but he was still curious and disturbed about where the sound of the crying baby had come from. He was also concerned about how few members had come to church and the fact that even they hadn't arrived on time. He knew that God had to stir the minds of the people somehow, but he didn't know how or when that would take place.

Early Monday morning, one of the brothers came to Reverend Lon's house with the tragic news that a church member's house had caught on fire. Not only had they lost their home, but their three-year-old baby had died in the fire. As the brother was telling Reverend Lon about the member's tragic loss, Reverend Lon began to think back about the prayer from Sunday morning and the cry of the baby. He kept hearing that sound in the back of his mind, over and over again.

Over the next few days, many people heard about the fire and the death of the baby. This devastating incident really got the attention of the community. On the following Sunday morning, the house of the Lord was filled to capacity, and many of the members arrived with an obvious sense of urgency. When nothing else can get the attention of God's people, God can!

CHAPTER 16

A True Act of Nobility

In all things shewing thyself a pattern of good works: in doctrine
shewing uncorruptness, gravity, sincerity; Sound speech that
cannot be condemned; that he that is of the contrary part
may be ashamed, having no evil thing to say of you.
—Titus 2:7–8

Reverend Lon Evans was a man of honor and integrity. He was well respected not only among his peers but by anyone who came into his presence. He was a truthful, reliable man who kept his word and followed through with his promises. If he said he was going to do something, it was going to get done. He conducted himself with perfect decorum, and anytime he was out in public, he was neatly and stylishly attired. No matter where he went, he continued to be a vessel for the kingdom of God.

Besides preaching the gospel of Jesus Christ, Reverend Lon was also concerned about the welfare of people in general. He was the vice president of the regional NAACP chapter, and he believed in and stood up for equal rights—not only for people of color but for all humanity. He had a practice of standing up for what was right, regardless of who was committing the wrong.

In one instance, Reverend Lon was approached by a husband and wife whose son had been incarcerated for a crime of which they said he was not guilty. Reverend Lon didn't know the couple or their son, nor did he know whether the young man was guilty or innocent. Nevertheless, they believed Reverend Lon could help them, and they said to him, "We heard that when you pray, things happen."

Being a man of compassion, Reverend Lon went to the prison and talked with the young man. "Did you commit this crime?" he asked.

The young man answered, "Oh no, sir, I did not."

Reverend Lon said, "God is a just God. If you didn't commit this crime, then God will release you." He prayed with the young man and then went to talk with the prison warden about the young man's conviction. "Warden, can I leave a prayer here for the entire prison?" he asked.

The warden replied, "Yeah, sure, go ahead." Little did he know that Reverend Lon was praying not just for the inmates but for the warden as well. God heard the prayer of His servant, and later the young man was released from prison. What a mighty God!

Reverend Lon was also a generous man who would give not only his time but also his money to help others. When people needed financial assistance, Reverend Lon would use his own credit to get a bank loan. Sometimes the money was never repaid, but that didn't stop him from helping someone else. He earnestly believed that as long as he helped others, God would take care of him and his family. We are reminded from Acts 20:35, "In everything I did, I showed you that by this kind of hard work we must help the weak, remembering the words the Lord Jesus himself said, It is more blessed to give than to receive."

Reverend Lon played a vital role in not allowing racial segregation of black students in schools in that community. He volunteered his time to visit the schools and make sure, as much as possible, that all the students were safe, treated humanely, and receiving the same educational privileges. Even when his two youngest daughters were involved in racial segregation, Reverend Lon demonstrated courage as he pressed forward for equality.

CHAPTER 17

The Last Days

His Lord said unto him, Well done, good and faithful servant.
—Matthew 25:23

As Reverend Lon Evans got older, he continued pastoring the church and conducting revivals. At times he was unable to drive himself, so his younger daughters—JoAnn, JoNell, Mellova, and Syretta—would drive and accompany him from town to town for the various services.

In 1967, Reverend Lon's health began to fail. He knew that his time of departure was near, for the days had begun to close and the night to fall. He still preached the word, although he was no longer able to stand on his own. He would sit down in the pulpit, or sometimes on the floor in front of the pulpit, to preach and teach the Word of God.

Eventually Reverend Lon went to Lubbock, Texas, to live with his oldest daughter, Doris Ray, who wanted to help her mother take care of her father. He began to suffer more health complications, but he didn't find it necessary to go to the hospital. Holding on to his faith, he believed that God would work a miracle for him.

On January 11, 1970, during a routine visit, Johnnie, the youngest son, saw that his father's health had further declined. He asked his father, "Do you want to go to the hospital?"

Reverend Lon replied, "For everyone's benefit, it would be best for me to go." He didn't want his family to be held accountable of negligence if anything happened to him while in their care. So Johnnie called for an ambulance to take his father to the hospital.

After arriving at the hospital, Reverend Lon told his son that the doctors might want to operate on him, but that they would find themselves unable to do so. It seemed as if Reverend Lon, just like Paul, knew that his time had come. "For I am now ready to be offered, and the time of my departure is at hand" (2 Timothy 4:6).

As they continued to talk, Johnnie asked, "Is there anything you'd like to say or forgive anyone of?"

Reverend Lon replied, "No, I do not. Don't you worry. I'll be fine. Just take care of Mae and the other little children." As the nurses rolled him through the double doors of the hospital, Reverend Lon looked at his youngest son for the last time and waved goodbye.

A few minutes later, the doctor came back out and said, "We weren't able to do anything for him. He just went straight to sleep."

Then a phone call was made to Mae, who had always been by her husband's side, and the family that the Lord had come for His servant, Reverend Lon Evans. He was a faithful servant until the end.

John recorded these words in Revelation 2:10: "Be thou faithful unto death, and I will give thee a crown of life." This is what Reverend Lon did, and he had finished the work that God had for him to do. "I have fought a good fight, I have finished my course, I have kept the faith" (2 Timothy 4:7–8). Reverend Lon Evans held on to his faith even to the last days!

CHAPTER 18

That Day Is Here: My Surreal Moment

My flesh and my heart faileth: but God is the
strength of my heart, and my portion forever.
—Psalm 73:26

No matter how prepared I thought I was for the news of my father's passing, I was very sorrowful and didn't want to come face-to-face with that surreal moment. Yes, I had known and understood that the day would eventually come, because death is inevitable, but suddenly it was reality—not just a dream.

Throughout our lives, my father had spoken with us about that day coming. He would say, "One day I will be gone back with the Lord, and I want you all to carry on the work. Stay saved, and don't stray away from what you've been taught. Holiness is right!" We had all moved to different cities where he knew there were many doctrines and teachings against holiness. He taught us that even though someone might testify that they're saved, sanctified, and filled with the Holy Ghost, that doesn't mean they're living in a holy way. Matthew 7:20 says, "Wherefore by their fruits ye shall know them."

He would tell my mother to stay with the church, no matter what. Sometimes after the death of the founder and pastor of a church, his wife is neglected and no longer recognized for all the sacrifices she has made. But my father encouraged my mother that she would be all right and could handle whatever might come her way. He told her, "God will take care of you and the girls."

On the evening of my father's death, my family and I traveled home to be with my mother. Along the way, I reminisced about all the things my dad had shared with me.

When we arrived at home, my mother opened the door and said in a soft, sad voice, "He's gone."

I hugged her and assured her, "You will be all right, and we're all here for you."

My mother replied, in a voice that sounded like she had been crying, "I'm going to miss him. His presence around here made me feel good."

Hearing and seeing my mother grieving for her husband and my dad made me feel heartbroken and sad, but once again I assured her, "You won't be alone. All your family and children will be here for you."

The day of my father's funeral was very difficult on all of us. As I sat there during the funeral service, all I could think about was that my father was actually gone. He was no longer with us, but I knew that he was with the Lord. "We are confident, I say, and willing rather to be absent from the body, and to be present with the Lord" (2 Corinthians 5:8).

Upon arriving at the cemetery, we each were given flowers to put on his casket. As we said our final goodbyes, it still felt so surreal that my father was no longer with us. Then I remembered what he had said to us one day: "In order to see me again, you have to live right and come to heaven." Yes, that day had come, but God gave us strength. Even though my father was gone to be with the Lord, we'll never forget all that he taught us. I shall forever cherish my fond memories of my father.

CHAPTER 19

The Legacy Continues

A good man leaves an inheritance to his children's children.
—Proverbs 13:22

Even after his passing, Reverend Lon Evans's teachings continued to be a paramount factor in the lives of his beloved wife and nine living children. The teachings of the devoted husband and father drew everyone who had known him closer together, ultimately proving the greatest purpose of Reverend Lon's life. Those who knew and loved Reverend Lon believed that while death can take away the body, it cannot destroy the loving memories created by the individual's life. "The Lord knoweth the days of the upright: and their inheritance shall be forever" (Psalm 37:18). Those memories are cherished and preserved through the hearts and minds of their loved ones.

Reverend Lon's family continued his legacy through ministering to God's people. In 1982, his third child, Pastor C. D. Evans, picked up the torch and continued his father's work by becoming the pastor of Wilson Chapel Church of God in Christ. Pastor Evans is dedicated to following God's voice and direction for the church. Years after his father's death, Pastor Evans and the congregation decided to step out on faith. They talked with the previous owners of the land, which had been given to the church, about erecting a new church building next to the original edifice. The previous owners gladly accepted the idea and said they would love to see a new church building down the hill from their homes. From that moment on, the church members knew they could always depend on the support of the previous landowners.

As Pastor Evans worked on the vision for the new church building, God told him to call upon the young people who had grown up in the church to help keep the vision alive. When he met with the young people and told them what God had said, they accepted the word and begin to work faithfully. In 1998, the new building was completed and Pastor Evans's vision became a reality. Two supportive members of the church made a generous donation,  which was just the beginning of the overflow of blessings that the ministry continued to receive.

Reverend Lon's youngest son, Superintendent Johnnie Evans Sr., continues his father's legacy by preaching the gospel and praying for people everywhere. Residing in Lubbock, Texas, he contributes to his father's legacy by supporting his brother at Wilson Chapel Church of God in Christ. For over four decades, he has come back to the Leon County community to preach the annual homecoming service on the fourth Sunday in July.

The daughters of the late Reverend Lon and Mary Evans—Doris, Ruby, Alma, JoAnn, JoNell, Mellova, and Syretta—are carrying their parents' legacy forward by staying with the church and supporting one another, just as their father wished for them. Because of their unfailing dedication to the ministry and their father's principles of holiness, the Evans family is blessed. "The just man walketh in his integrity: his children are blessed after him" (Proverbs 20:7).

Alma J. Evans-Fanniel

From top left: C. D. Evans, Alma J. Evans-Fanniel, Johnnie Evans Sr.
Middle: Doris Dixon (deceased), Ruby J. Evans Hall (deceased), JoAnn
    Weatherspoon
From bottom left: JoNell Braggs, Mellova J. Davis, Syretta Evans

CHAPTER 20

Unforgettable Memories

Many people could attest to experiencing the miraculous works of Reverend Lon Evans, but a few people who were close to his heart could testify to his love for God, humankind, and his family. Being a God-fearing man, he made sure to instill those same values within his nine children. The Evans children were taught to love God and work hard in all that they did throughout their lives. Reverend Lon taught his family to love one another, treat each other with respect, and appreciate each other on a daily basis. This type of upbringing made them a very close family.

Every morning, Reverend Lon would greet his wife and each of his children with "Good morning!" They would respond to one another with "Good morning! How did you sleep?" Every morning, they looked forward to telling each other about their dreams. After saying their morning prayers, and telling each other about their night, it was time for breakfast, which was a family event in the Evans household. You could smell the cooking of bacon throughout the entire house. Fresh eggs were gathered from the chicken coop and fresh milk from the cow. Yes, everyone from the youngest child to Reverend Lon himself played a part in preparing breakfast. This was bonding time for the Evans family.

After breakfast, it was time for work. Everyone except Mae, who stayed home to attend to the house, would head out to the business of growing crops and raising livestock. Their activities included feeding the animals, milking the cows, plowing the grounds, planting and harvesting the crops. They would typically do this work Tuesday through Friday, because Mondays were usually a day of rest for the Evans family.

They would all work until noon and then break for lunch. If work was close to home, they would eat lunch there, but if not, they would sit under a big shade tree for lunch and rest. After their lunch hour, they all would return to work, which continued until around five thirty, but no later than six o'clock.

When they got back home, everyone would take a bath. Mae would already have the table set and dinner prepared for the family. Dinner was always a hearty meal, often including fried chicken, chicken and dumplings, peas, beans, collard and mustard greens, corn, rolls, and cornbread. For dessert, she would have berry cobbler or peach cobbler, buttermilk pie, and a pound cake.

As everyone gathered around the table, Reverend Lon insisted that no one begin eating until everyone was seated. Then he would say grace, giving thanks for the food that was about to be received. At the end of grace, he would say, "The Lord is my shepherd, I shall not want" (Psalm 23). After dinner, the day would soon come to an end. Before bed, they would have prayer as a family and wish each other a blessed and good night.

Another of the many great memories for the Evans children was spending time with their father on the weekends. From Friday until Sunday night, the Evans family spent most of their time at church, but they made sure to take time for unforgettable family trips to the Texas towns of Bryan and Madisonville.

As Saturday arrived, the nine Evans children would be ecstatic, because every Saturday afternoon, Reverend Lon would take them to a popular burger spot in town. They always knew what day it was when they drove up to the burger spot and walked toward the back of the store for a huge, delicious homemade burger with a soda.

At home, they would go outside and play, practice singing or playing instruments, or read. They were taught to share with each other, no matter what it was. If one of the brothers or sisters knew how to do something, they would teach it to everyone else. Superintendent C. D. Evans would play the guitar, and his dad, Reverend Lon, would tell him to teach his brother and sisters what he was playing.

As the weekend would come to a close, it was time for everyone to get some rest and take time for conversation. Reverend Lon believed in the importance of everyone getting enough rest. Then, sitting in the living area, they would talk about various things, from the weekend to how amazing church had been on Sunday. Yes, the Evans family made many unforgettable memories that they will cherish for the remainder of their lives.

CHAPTER 21

The Final Call: In the Words of Alma Jean Evans-Fanniel

My mother, Mary Esther Evans, was the matriarch of the Lon Evans family. She loved her husband and family, but most importantly, she loved the Lord. She was saved, sanctified, and filled with the Holy Ghost. She was a great encourager and supporter for the work of the Lord. Even after the death of her husband, she continued working in the church and for the Lord. She always encouraged her children in the ministry. She respected God's people and never spoke negatively about anyone, even if they were not living a godly life. She would often say, "Don't put your mouth on the man of God, not even if they are living a ragged life. Let the Lord handle it." She was always careful about what she said, because she feared God and knew what He would do in love or reprimand when appropriate. "If you search my life," she'd say, "you'll not find anything." Her closing words were "Watch my life," meaning that there was nothing ungodly there to talk about.

As the years passed, my mother's health began to decline. While attending a Sunday church service on November 25, 2001, I received a phone call from the nursing home letting me know that my mother was not doing well. My sister and I drove to the nursing home to find her in grave condition, but I didn't want to believe that was how my mother would leave me. While at the nursing home, I decided to play one of my mother's favorite prayers by Bishop C. H. Mason. As she listened to the prayer, she responded with a few positive movements and repeated the words, "Yes, Lord," which made me hope that she was getting better.

Several hours later, after leaving the nursing home, I received notice that she had been transported to a local hospital. My sister and I drove to the hospital, where I was finally able to grasp the reality that those were the final  moments that I would spend with my mother. My sister and I sat there for some time, but finally we were told to go home because it was expected that our mother might get better.

Later that night, I received the final phone call that I had always known, deep within my heart, would one day come. It was the call that no one ever wants to receive. It was the call to tell me that my mother had transitioned from this life to a life with the Lord. "We are confident I say and willing rather to be absent from the body, and to be present with the Lord" (2 Corinthians 5:8). Yes, my mother left a lasting impression, both naturally and spiritually, that was sure to help carry all her children on after her death.

Afterword

My sincere purpose for writing this book was to tell my father's story. I wanted to gather and record actual accounts of miracles and healings associated with his ministry. My goal has been to share my father's spiritual greatness and how God worked through him as a man of faith. Certainly, we can all be encouraged and inspired when we read about unleashed faith in God and God's willingness to answer the prayers of anyone who will never doubt Him. My father's life is a testimony that God can and will use ordinary people who are fully committed to Him. Because of the many lessons my father taught me, I have been able to live my life in a strong relationship with God and with an unwavering faith in Him. My father's example has served me well, empowering me to be an independent person, a submissive wife, and a loving mother.

Looking back, I remember being a child and witnessing the great works of my father, a true soldier in the kingdom of God. I was instilled with my father's values. I learned how to pray, fast, and be a responsible person. My father was the perfect model, in his daily life with my mother, of how a man should treat a woman. I was taught by my father to have integrity, respect for myself and others, and love for everyone. I am the woman I am today because of the Lord. The parenting I received from Reverend Lon and Mary Evans was yet another extension of God's love toward my siblings and me.

Reverend Lon Evans was a truly noble man and a first-class citizen. His contributions to the community in which he lived, pastored, and ministered are still being realized and appreciated today. He left his mark on many other people, and his life demonstrated his love for God and his heart for the welfare of the people.

Congratulatory Remarks

Bishop Frank E. Fanniel Sr.

The completion of Alma Jean Evans-Fanniel's book, *Faith Walk: My Father's Story*, clearly illustrates how a dream becomes reality. After much prayer and a commitment to fulfill her mother's strong desire, she was able to complete this great task.

In this book, she shares with the world her father's outstanding ministry and accomplishments. She did an awesome job remembering all that she had experienced and witnessed. She reminds us how essential faith is needed in our everyday lives. She reveals to the readers how we will sometimes walk into unfamiliar places, but we have to trust where God will take us. "For we walk by faith, not by sight" (2 Corinthians 5:7).

I believe this book is going to be a blessing to every person who reads it. It was a great feat that required courage, determination, and perseverance. I commend and congratulate my wife, Alma Jean Evans-Fanniel, for a job well done!